THINK SIMPLE CLEVER SERIES

S.T.A.R.T. MARKETING FOR SUCCESS

HOW TO CREATE A STRONG MARKETING PLAN AND STICK WITH IT

LISA WOODWARD

1

For permission requests, write to **Lisa@icingmarketing.com**

The views expressed in this publication should be taken as
those of the author alone. Where real examples are
referenced, they are for the purpose of illustration and no
misrepresentation is intended.

Author's business website
www.icingmarketing.com

Book and Cover design by the author

First Edition: NOV 2021

ISBN Number: 9798759735595

10 9 8 7 6 5 4 3 2 1

"This book was born out of a blog I wrote when networking heavily during my early consultancy days. Often a kickstart for new businesses, as well as an important lifeline of support for any small operation, I found that networking groups frequently presented us all with an abundance of generous advice and offers. However, with limited resources to spare, how could anyone be sure of focusing their efforts in the right place – no matter how good a deal was being put forward?

I have written 'S.T.A.R.T. Marketing for Success' to help organisations unravel the avalanche of information and offers available to them, and to ensure their chosen promotional activities fit with a strong and realistic marketing strategy - that is in harmony with their brand purpose - to set them up for success."

Lisa Woodward

CONTENTS

FOREWORD

Businesses have never been under so much pressure. Managing the complexity of the modern world, they must continually find ways of adapting to shifts in human behaviour and modes of business operation. And with the current pace of change and technology we face, there is unlikely to be much let up. The weight of this will no doubt continue to increase with continually challenging commercial conditions and marketers will be on the front line. They have much to manage and deliver, but their budgets are often the first to get cut when the going gets tough. Having a strong well thought out and measurable marketing plan, that ensures marketing spend and effort are directed where it matters, is absolutely vital for business survival.

Before my move to consultancy, I had the luxury of corporate processes and templates to keep me in check, but the reality is we are all human and amidst the day-to-day immediacies of our day jobs, it can be hard to devote the time needed for structured thinking and planning. Templates become a tick box activity to remove from the to-do list and it can be all too easy for us to become lost in the daily clutter and wind up doing what we've always done - simply because there is no time to re-think. Worse still, there may be a temptation to jump on the latest marketing idea without being clear about how it will support specific marketing objectives. This culminates in organisations undertaking activities that appear to present a good opportunity, without being clear **why** they make sense for their particular business and brand. This is where time and money risk being either wasted or diverted from where it is actually needed.

My own marketing background, prior to setting up my consultancy business in 2012, includes over 20 years in the corporate world, so I am well versed with the art of structured planning, and actually rather enjoy it. For those less enthusiastic, please rest assured that marketing planning doesn't have to be complicated. With some simple structured thinking, you will be able to start out with a strong focused plan, which will give you much more chance of a successful year END.

As a trainer and coach, I recognise that it is not enough to shout about this from the rooftops. People have their own agendas and need help finding answers themselves, as well as straightforward methods and tools to implement those answers. This is where my S.T.A.R.T. process comes in.

The S.T.A.R.T. model presented in this book is a simple step by step process that facilitates marketing planning. Enabling businesses to get started on the right foot both on and offline, it ensures nothing important falls off the radar. By investing the time up front, it ultimately saves you time and money - by prioritising the right marketing channels and activities to reach your target audience.

To be great marketers, we need many skills and traits, and I firmly believe one of those is **perseverance**. Of course, we also need to be flexible and adaptable, but if we are single minded about what we want to achieve, we will be able to work through the daily noise, implementing and adjusting our marketing plans, without losing sight of the **end goal**.

PART 1

INTRODUCTION

In a world where so much knowledge is available literally at our fingertips, organisations face an abundance of information and advice, not to mention a constant barrage of unbeatable offers. Confronted by so much noise, how do you unravel what is presented to you and decipher what will best serve your organisation? Where should you focus your attention and finite resources?

Start with the End in Mind

In Stephen Covey's renowned book, "The Seven Habits of Highly Effective People", he reminds us to 'start with the end in mind' and this couldn't be more poignant in the context of marketing. Let's use the analogy of driving a car, to illustrate this. When we get in a car we already know where we want to go. There's not necessarily a fixed route to take and some routes will inevitably be better than others, but we always (hopefully) have an end destination in mind! Experience shows that when it comes to marketing within organisations, people can easily be distracted by new ideas and unmissable deals, thereby losing sight of the bigger picture and that destination point. This is most common when marketing projects are seen in isolation instead of being part of a larger plan and roadmap. When it comes to marketing planning, it is important to know your journey's end - i.e., what you are trying to **achieve.** Only then can you define which direction to take.

The day-to-day chaos and pressures of running a business can undoubtable result in planning being pushed aside. Or worse still, planning is recognised as something that needs doing, but becomes a going-through-the-motions operation to 'get out of the way'. This will result in a lazy plan that simply repeats what has been done before without much in-depth strategic thought. We have all heard the saying "insanity is doing the same thing over and over and expecting different results". This is usually attributed to Albert Einstein and although debate surrounds the authenticity of the original quote, it certainly rings true when it comes to marketing planning!

Another common issue is the tendency to get sucked into other people's advice as to what has worked for them in the past, or to aimlessly follow what the competition is doing. By all means listen, observe, and absorb, but before following the latest trend or playing copycat, consider how those activities could help **you** reach **your** end destination and achieve **your** specific business goals. (For instance, if you have identified the need to build credibility for your products or services, there would be little point in spending all your resource on driving traffic to your website until you've accumulated and uploaded some credentials. This could include testimonials, case studies, press coverage, awards, or any relevant accreditations).

There are never enough hours in the day or '£'s in the bank, so a single-minded approach to structuring and prioritising your marketing activities is key. An underrated skill for anyone developing and implementing a marketing plan is the ability to develop their **inner stubbornness**! Don't get me wrong, I am not suggesting organisations become inflexible, quite the contrary. In a constantly changing environment we need to continually check

11

we are following the right direction and may well need to adapt en route (just as when driving you may suddenly be faced with a huge traffic problem and need to take an alternative road). However, having sight of that end destination is important for assessing all the relevant options and making the right decisions for your organisation.

A Simple Approach

This is where my S.T.A.R.T. process comes in. Based on well recognised textbook theory and standards, I developed this approach to unravel the complexity of marketing and to guide organisations through their planning step by step. This methodology is applicable whether you operate as a solopreneur or as part of a larger team with sufficient resource to seek support from others.

The output is a strong marketing plan that best sets up your organisation for success, based on solid foundations and realistically recognising your resources and capabilities (including limitations). The process covers goal setting and activity planning, as well as tips on how to manage an effective implementation of the plan.

S.T.A.R.T. is a simple acronym that stands for:

12

SITUATION

ANALYSIS   Before you can set the path ahead, it is important to gain a clear understanding of what is happening today. Both from an organisational perspective and a broader external viewpoint.

THEMES   From your situational analysis, what are the themes you notice? What are the opportunities you can maximise and what issues need addressing? This will help to set your organisation's destination.

ACTIONS   Once your destination is set, it's time to identify your route options, looking at both the general direction (strategy) and specific activities.

RESOURCES   Next you need to make the plan happen, prioritising activities and managing anyone you need to bring on board to support the process.

TIMING   Finally the 5-step process looks at timing – how to plan your activities and track them to ensure there is no slippage in timing that could impact the delivery of other core activities.

Part of the 'Think Simple Clever' series

The idea for this series comes from my experience of providing marketing training to clients. The area they often find most useful is, not so much the theory but, the guidance through simple ideas and templates where they can apply their learnings to their own organisation. For me, this is a key component to any successful training as the client always knows their world best. Yet many business books focus on theory and examples, without providing the specific step by step guidance and tools to enable readers to apply the theory directly to their unique situation. The 'Think Simple Clever' series of marketing guides is where traditional marketing books meet modern training programmes.   You, the reader and expert in what you do, will always do the thinking, while I remain by your side to guide you through the process. Providing the right questions to extract the unique expertise you and your team have about your own organisation. Once you become more familiar with the S.T.A.R.T.

model, you will no longer need this book to follow the process. Its memorable acronym will keep you on track.

How to use this book

I have covered some basic theories and illustrated them with examples, but the focus of this book is on breaking down those theories into small manageable steps, that allow you to think cleverly about your organisation.

In each section, you will find practical tips, alongside planning templates and tools to assist you in gathering your thoughts. This approach works because you know your organisation and capacity best. With some systemised prompting, you will be able to find ways to reach your target audience that are within your means and capabilities.

The templates referenced are provided in a useful Word workbook, which will allow you to work directly on your marketing plan preparation. This free workbook can be accessed at: **https://www.icingmarketing.com/start**

Finally, to ensure you have understood each step of the process, each chapter will conclude with

15

reminder points – giving you a short summary of the main ideas you have just learnt.

This is just the S.T.A.R.T.

As you set off to S.T.A.R.T. your marketing activities with a strong plan, please remember that this is just the beginning. The way in which you execute and implement your plan will be critical for success, and that includes how you present and communicate your brand. A winning plan needs backing with a persuasive brand to ensure each marketing activity stand outs with consistency and connects with your ideal customer. If you don't achieve this, then no matter how much work and resource you put into your marketing, you may well struggle to gain traction and accomplish your goals.

A successful brand is one that can articulate a proposition that is unique to its organisation and relevant to its customers. To do this an organisation must be able to imagine its own values, principles and product or service benefits as seen through its customers' eyes – considering the messages they want to hear and the brand personality that would appeal to them. If this is a currently a weak area and you feel your brand lacks clarity, relevance or stand-out, you may need to address this as a housekeeping

16

activity in your plan. The key is to avoid putting it aside for later, because to bear fruit, a strong marketing plan must be accompanied by a persuasive brand.

PART 2

'S' = SITUATION ANALYSIS

Where are you now?

A successful marketing plan is one that has been thought out carefully, with clear goals. To avoid setting yourself up for failure, and thereby wasting valuable resources, you need to set realistic and achievable aspirations that still retain enough ambition to make an impact. Kick off by gaining an understanding of where you are today: What is the current situation both internal to your organisation and surrounding you in the external environment? You are headed on a journey, but you need to know where you are now to work out which roads you can take and where the hold ups might be. What's needed for this is known as a 'situation analysis'. Whether planning a start-up or running an existing large business, this step is your starting point to winning and should never be skipped before deciding on the strategy ahead.

You may have already set out long term aims for your organisation, so from this analysis you will be able to view things more deeply, to identify where the current gaps lie and to uncover the potential for more opportunities that can be developed. If you have a new business and are just getting started with your planning, this first step is vital for seeing the wood for the trees and identifying where you sit within your sector - highlighting both positive factors that you can exploit, and issues you need to address to mitigate any risks.

There are various models you can use to do this analysis. Your **choice** of technique is not particularly important. What counts is putting aside the time to **do** the analysis. It is all too easy to be get caught up in busy day to day operations, but if you don't take time to assess where you are today, you could set off blindly on the wrong course.

One of the most commonly referenced tools is a SWOT analysis, which takes me right back to my medieval student days. As abstract as it felt in my cosy bubble of learning, I have continued to use the SWOT model throughout my career, because of its simplicity and the way it provides an umbrella view of many factors affecting an organisation whatever its size.

What is a SWOT analysis?

The word SWOT is an acronym that stands for **S**trengths, **W**eaknesses, **O**pportunities and **T**hreats.

Your **S**trengths and **W**eaknesses are factors that are internal to your organisation such as product advantages, resources, finances, and any intellectual property etc. They are things over which you have some element of **control** - even if it doesn't always feel that way. For example, a weakness could be a particular employee in a different department who does not report to you. You may feel that this is out of your control, but actually it may just be **difficult** for you personally. You could contact their manager and negotiate how to deal with the situation. So technically, the situation is within the control of the organisation.

Opportunities and **T**hreats are factors that are happening externally in the wider marketplace and may impact on your organisation. Examples include

21

competitors, shopping trends or laws and regulations. **O**pportunities are possibilities you could exploit or areas that could be developed to your advantage. **T**hreats could have a negative bearing on your organisation and need to be mitigated to protect you. How these are interpreted can sometimes be subjective since a threat could also be seen as an opportunity, depending on how it is managed. For example, a new piece of legislation could be viewed as a threat creating barriers to work or more paperwork and cost. However, if your organisation is small, flexible, and therefore able to react quickly and get 'ahead of the game' before the competition, it could be seen as an opportunity to drive competitive advantage. Whichever way you look at these factors, the key denominator is that they are happening **out of your control** as an organisation.

All these elements are usually captured and presented in a two-way grid, as shown later in this chapter. There is also a version you can use in the S.T.A.R.T. downloadable **workbook.**

WHO should be involved?

Whether working solo to build your analysis, or brainstorming with a wider team, you will gain more from the process if you seek several perspectives to thoroughly investigate all the internal and external influences. You should also incorporate any research findings including your own desk research, as well as interview anyone not attending who could provide a useful perspective. Organisation founders and leaders should be heavily involved in the process, along with a selection of staff from different functions – from marketing to customer service and product development. Sometimes businesses may also seek external input from their clients or suppliers. If your organisation is in its infancy and doesn't have a team of staff, you should still perform a SWOT analysis with third party viewpoints. You could ask your accountant, suppliers or seek support and views from local networking groups.

After collating your background research and appointing your SWOT team, you will need to put aside a couple of hours for the brainstorm meeting. It may be useful to distribute any research findings in advance as background reading. Once gathered in the meeting, allow everyone to quietly collate their thoughts and ideas on sticky notes. This gives everyone the chance to voice their opinion without being overshadowed by more dominant or vocal members of the meeting. One thought per sticky note. Next, collect all the sticky notes and place them on a wall, clustering similar thoughts and ideas

23

together.   At this point you can invite further discussion if the sticky note wall sparks more ideas.

Brainstorms can become overwhelming if too many people are invited as they risk some viewpoints being missed unless the brainstorm is very carefully facilitated to extract everyone's views. Make your selection of attendees carefully. Everyone involved should have the time and opportunity to contribute, so be sure to invite comment from less outspoken personalities.

How to create your SWOT analysis

The following questions may be useful in igniting the conversation to gather relevant information. This is by no means an exhaustive list and some questions may seem more relevant than others for your sector so feel free to ignore any that don't make sense for your organisation / industry. Ensure all ideas generated are treated as valid and avoid vagueness by challenging everyone to be as specific as possible.

1. INTERNAL FACTORS

STRENGTHS: Remember when looking at the positive aspects of your organisation, you should include only those attributes that give you an **advantage** over other organisations. Avoid 'Brilliant Basics' which are the positive attributes that simply give you permission to operate in your sector. (These might include things such as customer service ratings or high-quality production if your competition also has these traits.) Ask yourself:

S1.   **What do you do well that others don't?**
S2.   **What processes are successful?**
S3.   **What brings in the best return?**
S4.   **What assets do you have that give you an advantage in what you do? (Customers, technology, patents, accreditations, cashflow, premises, location etc.)**
S5.   **What advantages do your team provide? (Knowledge, contacts, partnerships, reputation etc.)**
S6.   **What would customers / users say they like about your organisation?**

WEAKNESSES: Organisations can sometimes be blind to their own weaknesses, or even if they recognise them, they may not see them as serious or something that needs addressing. This is why it is so important to invite extra viewpoints. When working to identify your weaknesses, reframing questions from "what's wrong?" to "what could be better?" can encourage a more open and productive discussion. For instance:

W1. What could you do better? What could give you a better advantage over others?

W2. What processes could be improved?

W3. What assets does the organisation need? (Cash, equipment etc.)

W4. Where are the gaps in the team? How could the team be boosted? (Roles, skills, experience etc.)

W5. Are your premises appropriate? Is the location ideal for success?

W6. What would customers / users say could be improved?

2. EXTERNAL FACTORS:

This section takes a look outside of your organisation to identify areas you can play to your advantage and to recognise any market dynamics that could hinder your success. For a robust SWOT model, you should be ready to scrutinise colleague views to ensure opportunities are realistic and threats are substantiated so the size of risk is understood. For example, if you predicted a new emerging trend that 'might' take off, it would be important to recognise when it could realistically happen. If new legislation would be required for it to become a real possibility and would take years to come into effect, over investing in the opportunity in the short to medium term could take away valuable resource from addressing a more immediate threat to your success. The Office of National Statistics (ONS) (**https://www.ons.gov.uk**), which provides official data collated on behalf of the government, can be a useful free source of information when researching the external environment. The ONS is responsible for collecting and publishing statistics related to the economy, population, and society at a national level, as well as at regional and local levels.

You can also use other business models such as PESTELE to provide a structure for looking at your external influences (see point 3 in this chapter). And if you are a charity addressing a public issue, you will need to include the layperson's understanding of that issue (which could impact support and / or donations) as well as government policy makers' understanding (which could impact funding or policy change that would support the charity's cause).

OPPORTUNITIES: What factors could contribute to your success?

O1. **How is your market / sector growing and what are the trends that will help your organisation?**

O2. **What are your competitors' gaps? What are they not able to do, that you are?**

O3.   Is there anything in your market / sector that you could address? Are there any new areas emerging where your organisation could have an advantage?

O4.   Are there any regulation changes that could impact your organisation positively?

O5.   Are there any changes to supply and / or raw material pricing that could impact you positively?

O6.   Do customers think highly of you?

THREATS: When working through your threats, look at what you need to overcome and whether you should be introducing contingency plans or measures to reduce their effect?   A well mitigated threat can sometimes turn into an opportunity!

T1.   What are the trends that could hinder your success?

T2.   What are the barriers to your success?

T3.   Is there any new competitor activity such as new entrants or new developments with existing competitors?

T4.   Is there any risk to any aspect of your supply network and / or pricing?

T5.   Are there any changes in people's behaviour that could negatively impact your organisation? (Consumer trends, workplace

expectations etc.)
T6.   Is there any new legislation in your sector that could impact you negatively?
T7.   Could technology alter the way you need to do business?

3. PESTELE ANALYSIS:

This business framework (which builds on the old PEST model and is sometimes known as STEEPLE) focuses on identifying and monitoring any external influences and can be a useful input into the O and T of your SWOT analysis. Another anacronym, PESTELE stands for:

POLITICAL   Are there any political factors that could affect organisations and how they operate? They could include political stability or instability, government policy (trade, tax, overseas), labour law, environmental laws etc.

ECONOMIC   What is the economic situation and outlook ahead? This will inevitably have an impact on organisational success and customers' ability or willingness to spend / donate. Consider economic growth, disposable income, interest rates, exchange rates, inflation.

SOCIO-CULTURAL This is all about the population (growth, age distribution) and its shared attitudes towards topics which might include careers, health, and wellbeing. These are important for understanding societal expectations and what drives customer behaviour.

TECHNOLOGICAL With technology advancing at a fast pace, which innovations could affect your organisation? Will there be new ways to offer your products and services, or new ways to communicate them?

ENVIRONMENTAL It is no surprise that the environmental landscape is becoming increasingly important, with governments setting pollution targets and populations calling for more sustainability. Some of these factors could be classed under P or S, but regardless of how you classify them, they should be considered.

LEGAL   Which legal requirements are relevant to the way you operate? It is vital to keep abreast of any changes from health and safety, labelling and product safety, to advertising standards. And if you plan to export, be aware of local laws which may be different.

ETHICAL   This is a relatively new addition to the framework and relates to moral and ethical issues that could arise and must be managed. It considers fair trade, slavery acts, child labour and the general social responsibility of organisations.

4. USING THE MATRIX

Once you have removed any duplication of ideas, you may find it useful to present the information gathered in a two-way grid as follows. There is a blank grid provided for you to use in the downloadable **workbook**.

Sometimes there can be debate over which quadrant to place an idea; remember, S & W are factors over which you have some element of control, and O & T are not within your control.

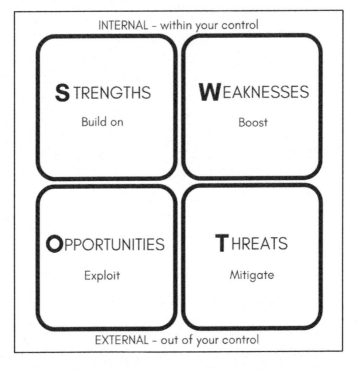

However, don't over think it. The key thing is to gain an overall understanding of factors that can impact favourably or against you. If you are an organisation that has been operating for a while, it is important to not assume you can continue to do your marketing in the same way as you have always done in the past.

In the next chapter, we will look at how to use the information presented in your SWOT matrix.

REMINDERS – SITUATION ANALYSIS:

Remember:

• **You can't set the course ahead unless you know where you are today.**

• **Use a technique such as a SWOT analysis to assess both positive factors you can develop and negative factors you can address or protect against.**

• **Sticky notes are useful for thought collection and then grouping into similar ideas.**

PART 3

'T' = THEMES

Find the themes

With your SWOT matrix complete, you can now look for any themes that stand out. What are the issues your organisation needs to address before it is able to progress, and can you spot any positions of leverage? This will help you set marketing objectives for your organisation, which we will address later in this chapter. Look at each of the SWOT quadrants and consider:

- How could you build your strengths and boost your weaker areas?

- Which opportunities could you exploit?

- Which threats must you tackle and how could you head them off?

- Are there any interconnections between the quadrants? E.g., How could your strengths be used to take advantage of the opportunities or to combat the threats ahead? Could any of the opportunities be used to minimise your weaknesses?

When you have asked yourselves these questions, capture the themes in a list.

Dig deeper

Now as you begin to unravel the information you have gathered, challenge your SWOT team to dig deeper to ensure nothing has been missed. This can be done by applying the principles of the Problem Tree analysis model, which can be a useful way to gain a clearer understanding of the strategic challenge you face. By dissecting your issues and openings further, this classic tool breaks down your findings into more manageable chunks and helps you uncover **why** they **matter.**

CONSEQUENCES

ROOT CAUSES

Imagine the issue you have found is the trunk of your problem tree and from that trunk grow the branches. These represent the consequences of that issue, and you need to determine whether you can live with them. If you can, should you ignore the issue and focus your efforts on something more important?

Also ask yourselves, whether you can you control the consequences. If the answer is no, what steps do you need to take to mitigate them? Essentially you need to decide what to let go of and where it is worth focusing your effort.

You should also delve deep underneath the trunk to find the root cause of the the issue. You may well need to address this rather than the issue that first presents itself.

For example, a fictional bakery business identifies a declining sales trend for a particular range of biscuits and, assuming they are no longer popular, decides to discontinue the range. This is despite the fact that this range has been more profitable than other products they make. With a bit of digging, the business discovers the cause for the lower popularity is due to a stock out in their busiest outlets which has reduced availability to purchase. A further dig reveals that the stock out has been caused by issues with one supplier who has been unable to provide a key decorative element for these biscuits. Armed with this new information, the business realises that rather than eliminating a lucrative range, they need to resolve the stock issue with the supplier, or if that's not possible, research whether alternative decorative elements would be as popular.

As you work through the causes and consequences, capture your list of true themes (those that need working on) in the template provided in the downloadable **workbook**. You can either do this with your entire SWOT team or, if some members have more relevant knowledge for certain subjects than others, you could break into subgroups.

Categorise the true themes

Faced with a long list of themes, it is now time to unravel and prune so that you can decide what to do with them! Whilst constantly referring back to the potential impact on the business, customer, or brand, take this list and notice:

- What is **not working**? What do you need to **STOP** doing?

- What **needs addressing**? What do you need to **START** doing?

- What **is working** that you need to **CONTINUE** and do more of?

STOP	START	CONTINUE

Use the template in the downloadable **workbook** to order your thoughts.

If your organisation has been operating for a while, it can be easy to adopt habits of doing the same as "we've always done" or to get drawn into meeting specific customer requests – because they pay the bills. You must, however, look beyond these influences and also consider the bigger picture – to ensure you support your organisational and brand objectives at the same time.

Set your Marketing Goals

Having categorised your themes, you should now formulate your goals for the next marketing period – i.e., what you want to achieve, *specifically*. If you can define what you are aiming towards, it will be much easier to see what you could do to move towards those aims. Your goals usually relate to the year ahead, but you should also look beyond this timeframe as there may be things you need to achieve *now* to allow you to reach a 3 to 5 year goal. Keep your goals succinct and don't have too many. Any more than 3 or 4 and you risk losing focus. Aim to do less, but better!

Setting out clear goals not only provides direction for the organisation, but also allows you to plan and then track how well you are performing. This direction also provides a permanent reminder so that you are not side-tracked by new ideas and special one-off deals. Let's be honest, it's easy to get distracted when faced with so many sources of advice and offers, especially when managing a low budget. Each marketing decision you make, however flexibly you wish to operate, should always relate back to one of your 3 to 4 goals. (We will discuss techniques for activity setting in the next chapter).

Imagine a young jewellery business that has no allocated advertising budget and whose usual 'strategy' is to purchase ad-hoc media deals when and as they come up. You may argue that having a marketing goal is not possible in this instance as it is simply a matter of waiting for media opportunities to arise. Not true! This type of flexible approach doesn't prevent them from having media goals. They should still define:

- who they want to reach

- the appropriate profile / image needed for their media choice

- the advertising company they want to keep (i.e.,

41

other brands they would be happy to sit and advertise alongside)

- when they want to advertise (i.e., are there any promotional periods that are particularly important to their plan?)

Armed with this clarity, they would be able to quickly sift through 'deals' as they occur and identify the opportunities that will better help them reach their goals, even if it means turning away something that, at face value, looks too good to miss based on price alone. Marketing budget allocated solely on value encourages you to spread yourself too thinly and is less likely to support you in achieving your goals.

For the true themes you have identified, set out your specific aims, by defining SMART goals. There have been various adaptations of the SMART model over the years – this is the one I prefer:

SPECIFIC What are you specifically aiming for? E.g., Rather than having a generic goal of 'increasing awareness', where are you trying to increase awareness? And to whom?

MEASURABLE   Quantify or at least suggest an indicator of progress to define how you will know if the goal has been met. It could be a finite outcome, or be measured as a percentage, frequency, rate, number   E.g. To increase awareness from X% to Y%.

ACHIEVABLE   This is to ensure your goal isn't too far-fetched. You need to have the resource to achieve it and there should be evidence of similar goals being met in the past by your or similar organisations. That said, I do believe your 'A' should also be **ambitious**. If goals are too easily achieved, people tend to be under motivated and achieve less.

RELEVANT   Goals should be appropriate to the individual or team and their job role. Or, at an organisational level, to the overall purpose and strategy of the organisation.

TIME-BOUND   A deadline creates a sense of urgency, so ensure your goals have

43

a time limit by which they should be reached. Longer term objectives should identify key milestones so that they are not put off or forgotten.

In recent years, some models have added 'ER' to become SMARTER. 'E' is for enjoyable which helps create enthusiasm and motivation to achieve the goal and 'R' is for respectful to ensure other people, roles, organisational processes and needs are taken into consideration.

Below are three examples of typical generic marketing goals and how they could be modified to become SMART – and thereby become more useful:

1. **Increase Market Share:** Market share is often measured as a sign of how you are performing against your competition. However, this goal is neither specific nor timebound. Would a 1% increase over 10 years be acceptable? Probably not. A SMART revision might be: ***Increase market share by 10% by year end.***

2. **Increase brand awareness on social media:** Whether you are a new company or an existing company launching a new product, increasing

44

brand awareness is a good marketing goal to consider since potential customers clearly need to know about you before they interact with you. Once again, this goal is not specific enough. How will you know that you have increased awareness? Just putting your company or product onto social media does not guarantee potential customers will notice you. A SMART revision might be: **Increase social media engagement by 25% by the end of the 2nd quarter**. By measuring engagement, you are able to judge whether people are noticing your posts in their feed and whether they are liking what they see enough to find out more or interact.

3. **Launch our new range of jewellery**. Companies may choose to grow business by launching a new product or service that builds on their existing brand awareness and loyalty. In this instance, how would you evaluate whether the time and effort put into the launch will have been worthwhile. Instead, a goal such as the following allows you to define what success looks like: **Launch the new range into 40% of our existing retail partners with supporting promotions by the year end.**

Use the template in your **workbook** to articulate your

45

SMARTER goals.

REMINDERS – THEMES:

Remember:

- Find the themes from your SWOT and dig deeper to find the root causes and consequences to ensure you find the 'true themes' on which to work.

- Decide what you need to STOP, START and CONTINUE doing.

- Set out 3 to 4 SMARTER goals to provide focus in your planning and to evaluate the effectiveness of your marketing activities.

PART 4

'A' = ACTIONS

Find your route options

Once your destination is set with clearly defined SMARTER goals, you are ready to plan your route. Going back to our original driving analogy, this means identifying the roads you need to follow to reach your destination (i.e. your goals). Stay broad at first without detail to decide what needs to be done 'directionally' – i.e., What are your strategies? Then think about the detail of what needs to be done.

Strategies sometimes get confused and / or interchanged with objectives. A useful way of structuring your thinking is to use the "To... By..." process:

OBJECTIVES are WHAT you want to achieve (E.g., **To....** increase marketing share by 10% by the end of the fiscal year). This is what you defined in part 3.

STRATEGIES are HOW you will achieve those objectives (E.g. **By** ..... promoting to a new type of customer or launching a new range).

If you are struggling to find manageable strategies, first think of all the things you **COULD** you do to meet your objective? Is there anything you have tried before that worked? Or is there anything you have tried before that you could do differently?

Don't worry about resources, knowledge, or time at this stage, as a more open mind will breed creativity. Keep your thoughts top level to avoid getting bogged down in the detail. You may find using one or more of the following techniques useful. These can all be worked on by yourself or in a brainstorm environment as you did earlier for the SWOT analysis:

REVIEW YOUR CUSTOMER TOUCHPOINTS

This technique involves looking at where your ideal customer MIGHT encounter your organisation along their purchasing journey with you:

- **Before purchase:** Where the customer could

become aware of your business and / or research you

- **During purchase**: Where customers see you and how they experience your business during the purchase process

- **After purchase**: Their experience with you post purchase

It is a good idea to first profile a 'persona' for your ideal customer as this will give you an understanding of them and the way they live, which can guide you in imagining places to reach them (see more on this in chapter 7).

I have often used this type of touchpoint model for auditing brands and checking their consistency of communication along the customer journey, but it is also ideal for generating marketing ideas. By listing as many potential customer touchpoints as possible, you will start to see opportunities for strategies that could reach your objectives.

For example, if you were trying to reach a new customer type, you would need to work hard in the 'pre-purchase' section of the model to find ways to increase their awareness of your products and services. If you did not yet know much about this new customer type, you might need to undertake research to find out more to allow you to position your pre-purchase communication appropriately. Simply 'increasing online presence' won't suffice. Awareness is only of use if it can lead to desire!

The illustration above (although not exhaustive) highlights some typical touchpoints for you to consider. However, try not to limit to the usual suspects – website, social media etc. Yes, you need to include these, but make sure you also go beyond the obvious and consider how this new customer spends their day, week, and month. This is where your customer persona profile comes in as it will help you build an image of where they go and what media they access so that you do not miss any potential touchpoints. Perhaps your target customer attends local fairs, which could be relevant for reaching them with your products. If that is the case, which fairs specifically would be most interesting for your products? (E.g., If you are selling high-end produce, you should ensure the fairs you attend attract other stalls of similar prestige and pricing.) Or, if your target customer commutes into a city for work, where could you reach them? You could choose to advertise on their journey, via free newspapers, train carriage poster ads or even on the stairs from the platform. Of course, this involves a reasonable sized budget, but a smaller leaner business could still apply the same principles, but in a more creative way. For example, a new café could design a treasure hunt chalked on the pavement to entice commuters in for their breakfast en route. This would only be appropriate if right for that café's brand, but if it was aiming to project a playful image, this could potentially be a novel approach for standing out as well as being simple to execute. And so on.......

Please note that this way of thinking isn't reserved for consumer brands; business services should use the model too, because at the end of the day, there is still a human signing the contract. So where can you reach them? At trade events? At the gym near their work after hours?

Use the table in your **workbook** to capture your customer touchpoints and identify those that are most relevant and useful for reaching your marketing goals.

BEHAVE FAMOUSLY!

You could also imagine your organisation is a famous person or brand. Putting yourself in the mind of another can help lift limitations on your thinking. It can be difficult to be creative when we have our usual expectations in place – barriers such as budget or capacity. But these types of restrictions will always be there, and instead of hiding behind them, we need to force the brain to think in a different way. Taking what the brain thinks is fact and retraining it to remove those barriers and open up your thinking.

Choose 3 or 4 and imagine what they would do in your shoes. What would Richard Branson do to reach your goals? What would Apple do? You could even image how one of your competitors would behave? You may not have the budget of a famous brand and you may also feel their style would be totally wrong for your organisation ("we would never do it like that"), but the idea is to bring in some new direction and avoid always going down the same road. Once you overlay your own brand style, voice and resources, you may uncover some new and interesting approaches. If you were a travel agent, for instance, how would you behave if you were Apple? You would certainly disrupt and do things differently. Perhaps you could focus your attention on the creative industry to tap into a pool of opinion leading and influencing humans, who like to challenge the norm and talk about it. This would require you to look at the customer journey of someone in the creative industry to identity marketing strategies. (These might include sponsoring advertising or design award events. Of course, being "Apple", you wouldn't just plonk your logo on the awards agenda, you would have to come up with something more original!)

FAMOUS BRAND OR PERSON	HOW WOULD THEY **APPROACH** THIS OBJECTIVE?	WHAT **CAN I TAKE** FROM THIS?

Use this template (also in the **workbook** to capture your thoughts).

'WHAT IF' TECHNIQUE?

Most people are more creative in their thinking than they realise. However, in the context of a busy working schedule, practicalities, and previous experience of what does and doesn't work, (or even fear of the unknown,) can block that part of the brain. A simple, yet effective technique to push away those hindrances is the 'What If' technique. This allows people who struggle to push aside practical limitations to firstly acknowledge them, and then to brainstorm what they would do if those barriers weren't in the way. What would you do......

- **IF** you had a magic wand

- **IF** the market place wasn't so difficult to enter

- **IF** advertising wasn't too expensive,

- **IF** you had specialist knowledge

- **IF** you had more resource

- etc. etc.?

Use the 'What If' template in your **workbook** to

capture your ideas and then see if any ideas are generated that you could take on board or adapt.

WHAT ARE THE **BARRIERS?**	**WHAT IF** THAT BARRIER WASN'T AN ISSUE?

As you work through these techniques, you should keep in mind the classic **Four Ps** of Marketing. Much of the emphasis of marketing planning theory is on how to **promote** a product or service, however, the other three **Ps** should not be neglected. If there is a weak area in your SWOT analysis, can it be addressed through pricing? Do you need to change how the product offer is articulated...etc.? For the unindoctrinated, here is a summary of the 4 pillars of marketing:

PRODUCT: This is the product or service being **offered** which should connect to a need or want. You must be clear and be able to articulate what makes it unique before being able to market it successfully. See more about this in Chapter 7 (Be Customer Centric).

PRICE: Once you are clear on your 'offer', the price position should be set. It needs to achieve the margin appropriate to your business targets, but also consider the context and how it sits against competitor offers.

PROMOTION This is a huge area and looks at the many possibilities to promote your offer including advertising, public relations, social media, search engine marketing, events etc. Wherever you promote your offer you must be consistent and communicate a well thought out brand proposition to maximise success.

PLACE By place, the model is referring to 'where' you can present your product / service to your ideal customer. This is about where you distribute it both online and offline. Your offer should be easily found by your target customer and must be in keeping with the brand image. If you are selling through a third party, you should also consider the other brands sold by that party, and whether that has an impact on your own brand image.

Over time, some marketers have argued that this model should be extended to include a further four Ps, which promote closer working between marketing and other aspects of organisations (such as HR and technology). I don't necessarily agree that the new four P's need to be forced into this existing robust and simple marketing model that has been around for decades (and this would not be the place to discuss the full argument). However, these additional P's **ARE** important for organisational success and should certainly be reviewed.

PEOPLE: There is no point in having a perfectly positioned marketing strategy without the right people to deliver on your brand promise and experience. So as part of your marketing strategy, be sure to look at everyone working with you (internally and externally) and check there are no skills (or indeed chemistry) gaps.

PROCESS: Are the correct systems and processes in place to ensure your product / service can be delivered successfully to your customers?

PHYSICAL
EVIDENCE: How do you reassure your customers and provide proof that your organisation can deliver? The physical environment in which the customer experiences you will have an impact on how you are perceived.

PHILOSOPHY: What is the philosophy behind your organisation? Often referred to as your purpose, values, and mission. If your potential customers understand what makes your organisation tick and why you are in business, this will differentiate you and help you to stand out from the competition.

Prioritise and set the course

Using the above techniques, you should now have a

substantial list of options that you COULD undertake. Even the most resource abundant of marketing departments will struggle to find the time and budget to tackle everything. So, faced with a long list of options, it is only human nature to choose the easily achievable items and tick them off quickly. However, this tick-box approach can all too easily absorb us in low impact activities, leaving no time for the important items, that might take more time, thought, or effort, but that will ultimately make more of a difference to the organisation.

This means it is time to prioritise. Avoid wasting effort by focussing your energy, time and resources on the strategies that will be most significant in meeting your goals and leading to success. Their effectiveness will depend on the impact they may have, as well as on your ability to implement them well. Resources and capabilities will therefore play a role in this decision making process.

1. SCORING:
For each idea collated, consider how important they will be for reaching your marketing goals, combined with how difficult they will be to implement.

• Firstly, score the items out of 100 for impact – i.e., an item with a perfect score of 100 will be the most impactful in reaching your aims.

- Next, score each item out of 100 for difficulty. 100 being very difficult to implement and low numbers involving very little effort or resource.

- Finally, plot these scores on a prioritisation matrix as shown, to identify visually where to focus.

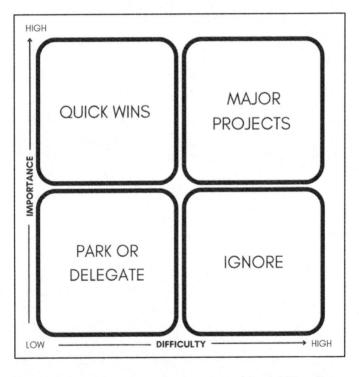

Note: The reason for using scores out of 100 rather

than say 10, is to avoid everything being too close together. Thus forcing you to rank high or low scoring activities against each other.

2. READING THE GRID:

You are essentially trying to balance what is achievable with what will increase your chances of reaching your goals.

1. **High Impact/Low Difficulty:** These are your QUICK WINS and the ideas you should look out for first. These are strategies you can approach with ease and that will be most effective.

2. **High Impact/High Difficulty:** These MAJOR PROJECTS are ideas that could have a high impact with the potential to provide a good return but could be complex and drain your time and resource. However, ignore these ideas at your peril! Just because they are difficult, doesn't mean they should be dropped. In the context of your marketing goals, you should consider whether these ideas are worth fighting for and, if they are likely to take a long time to achieve, look for the next steps needed to be taken, NOW and over the coming months, to set the path ahead for future success.

3. **Low Impact/Low Difficulty:** It is a common mistake to home in on the easy stuff in this quadrant – after all, who doesn't enjoy busying themselves and ticking items off their to-do list?! However, if the easy stuff only has low potential for impact, we risk becoming busy fools working on areas that take time and resource away from ideas that are more important for achieving success. PARK any items that fall here unless they are easily delegated. Since planning is an on-going part of running any organisation, you will be able to pick these up in future should their potential for impact increase.

4. **Low Impact/ High Difficulty:** Well, who wants to drain their energy on something that is difficult for very little gain? Ideas in this quadrant are quite frankly THANKLESS TASKS that will suck your energy and divert you from doing something more effective, so make sure you ignore them!

It should be noted that over time, market conditions and trends may change, so it is worth revisiting this matrix in the future to check whether everything is still relevant and sitting in the correct quadrant. See your **workbook** for the relevant template.

Identify the detail

Now for each strategy you have prioritised, break it down into the individual tasks and activities you need to undertake. What do you need to do to make these strategies happen? What is your action plan?

Don't worry at this stage If you feel your organisation can't manage all the actions. This process is about recognising what needs doing and where you may need to seek help externally. I will go into more depth in the next chapter where we look at allocating and managing resources.

As you develop your action plan, try to be as specific as possible and for larger actions, break them down into sub-tasks to make them feel more manageable. For example, for a solopreneur, developing a new website might seem like a huge project, so break it down into small steps such as:

- Research: identify site styles you like, what your competition is doing

- Brief: create the website brief (There is more on briefing in the next chapter)

- Define partners: if you are going to work with an external agency, research appropriate partners and agree budget

- Content: Develop the content – internally or with a copywriter

- And so on ....

Use the Actions Plan template in the **workbook** to capture detailed tasks. You'll notice there is also a column for priority which you can ignore now as we will discuss that in part 5.

OBJECTIVES (TO)	STRATEGY (BY)	CORE ACTIVITIES (DETAIL)	PRIORITY (1,2,3)

REMINDERS – THEMES:

Remember:

- Define strategies relevant for meeting your marketing goals.

- Be creative in your thinking to open more possibilities.

- Use a prioritisation matrix to decide where to focus your efforts in your plan.

P A R T   5

'R' = RESOURCES

Make the plan happen!

Of course, a great marketing plan will only be as good as its implementation, making effective management of your resources a key success factor. I frequently hear people talk about how much money they have available (or not) to spend, but we are talking about more than budget control. You will need to review and handle **all** your resources carefully: because to execute a plan well, you also need to look at people power including your own time and effort. This chapter covers tips for managing these resources effectively.

Prioritise your spend

Setting aside a specific marketing budget encourages you to plan your investment and avoid getting swept up in the latest offers. A generally accepted budget should be 5 % - 10% of turnover, although a start-up business entering a new market may initially need to over- invest. The reality of having a fixed budget usually means you face some form of spending limit, so rather than activating a little bit of everything, you are more likely to get noticed by your ideal customer and get traction by focusing on doing just a few things really well.

We spoke earlier about the four (then eight) Ps of marketing. Well, I believe there should be a nineth! All great marketing plans have to be carefully '**P**'rioritised, so that their owners can decide where it is most important to invest, particularly if business projections do not fully go to plan and you need to adjust your spending patterns.

I recommend allocating a priority number 1,2, or 3 to each activity in your marketing plan. By definition all the activities in your plan are a priority if you have followed the S.T.A.R.T. process methodically, as they all link back to your marketing goals. However, a priority system recognises where you have flexibility should you need it:

1 indicates the activity is top priority and absolutely **critical** to achieving the marketing goals set. They are time sensitive, and any reduction, cancellation or delay could have a detrimental effect on reaching your marketing goals.

2 is also of high importance and time sensitive, but other activities may be less dependent on them. You may still be able to reach all or some of your goals, however, there may be a delay in doing so.

3 is for activities that 'should' be undertaken and are reasonably stand-alone and non time sensitive. Removing them or delaying them will simply delay reaching your goals (or reduce your reach for now).

If anything changes that could affect your ability to undertake any part of your plan (such as new market conditions, a change in human resource, or a new but important opportunity that requires reallocation of resources), a priority system will help identify where to pull back and where to continue to focus. Your organisation will be able to understand what it absolutely **must** do to achieve its goals and what **could** be reduced or delayed if required. The last activities to drop should be the no.1 priorities. Flexing resource like this is better than making decisions based purely on finite cost as it considers timing requirements and activities that have a knock-on effect on each other.

If you face an uncertain market environment or cash flow restrictions, you may wish to choose to implement your marketing spend with caution and flexibility. In this situation, having a prioritisation system allows you to start the financial year with a focus on investing in only your most important activities (no.1's) and this is why a priority column has been included in the Actions Plan template in your **workbook**. After a while you can reassess the situation and decide whether you are able free up resource for the next level of activities (no.2's followed by no.3's). Staying adaptable is key to managing unpredictability and prioritisation keeps the end in sight while you navigate through this uncertainty.

Implementation through others

To make things happen, a plan is unlikely to unfold without the input of others. Whether engaging someone to undertake specific tasks on your behalf or to simply soften the path and provide support, it is important to recognise who you need to collaborate with for each project – from team members, different departments, or external companies – and how to engage them effectively.

1. STAKEHOLDER MAPPING:
A bit of a buzz word, Stakeholder Mapping identifies who can best support you in implementing a specific project. It can be tempting to work with people we get on with best, but a larger project can involve many people, so it is important to filter and concentrate on those who will have the best input. This involves looking at their level of **interest** in the project and their **influence** or **power**.

Of course, if you are employing the expertise of an external supplier, such as a design agency to create packaging design for a new product, they are likely to already be an interested party. In which case your main role is to check they have the right capability and credentials.   However, it is not only external support that can make or break a project. Using the same example, you will almost certainly need:

•   your finance team or accountant to be on board with the numbers

•   the production team (or production company) to ensure the packaging design can feasibly be

71

created in practice

- your legal contact to check labelling meets legal requirements

- and so on......

There are many people and / or departments you *'need'* to involve, but there are also others you *'could'* choose to consult to smooth the way forward. For example, continuing with the same example, you could invite the confidence of someone within the launch chain to provide valuable feedback or to act as an ambassador for the project. This could be anyone from the sales team, a trusted retail partner or even a client with whom you have already built a solid relationship.

Start by listing everyone who should or could be involved in the project. Once you have that list, look at their level of interest in that project versus their influence / power and plot them on the grid provided in the **workbook**. Use it as a visual reference to identify who to work with:

- PROMOTERS: Anyone who has a high level of interest AND the ability to influence, is key to your project so **invest most time here and manage them thoroughly.**

72

- POTENTIAL: Some stakeholders may not have much interest in your project but have the *potential* to be useful if you can get them on side. Keep them **satisfied and completely informed** to prevent them from becoming a **negative influence**. As in our earlier example, a salesperson who is not interested in selling on your new product (perhaps because it would involve more effort and time) could still directly influence the success of getting it listed with an important retail partner.

- INEFFECTUAL: You may find you have willing parties interested in your project and ready to help, but who have little influence. **Avoid spending too much time** with them at the expense of building more valuable relationships. However, you should still maintain their interest, by keeping them in the loop, and **monitor** them. If they become more influential and therefore more valuable to your project over time, you can increase the time you invest with them.

- ENERGY DRAINERS: **Minimise your efforts** with stakeholders who have little interest or ability to influence. Provide regular but little contact to keep them informed but avoid draining time and energy that could be directed more usefully.

73

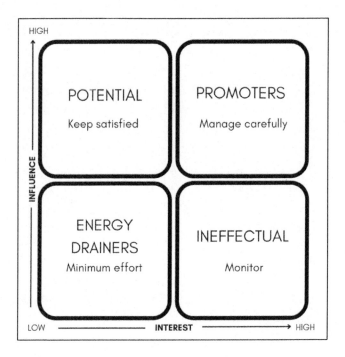

2. ENGAGE THEIR SUPPORT:

Having identified the stakeholders you need on board, you now need to inspire and secure their support. For those who already have a vested interest it will be easiest, but with all stakeholders you should show them how their involvement is relevant to them. The key here is to position your activities, and the input required from them, by talking about it from **their point of view**. This means recognising their needs and communicating how your activities help meet those needs, i.e., **What's in it for them?**

For example, let's consider the disengaged salesperson from our POTENTIAL quadrant earlier. They may be reluctant to put in the extra effort for a new unproven product launch if they can't see much gain for themselves. So, you could show research results that forecast strong sales performance that will help them reach their personal sales target, or demonstrate how the new product could provide leverage for a better shelf position for the whole range which would also boost sales and ultimately link to the salesperson's bonus. Positioned like this, your product launch suddenly becomes integral to meeting their own objectives. Avoid falling into the trap of merely listing your own marketing goals which may appear rather abstract compared to the salesperson's day-to-day reality and agenda.

This approach for engaging stakeholder support is just as relevant in less commercial roles too. If you were looking for celebrities or influencers to act as ambassadors for your charity, as brilliant as your cause may be, you still need to show the relevance to them personally, so they choose you over other worthy charities. Or maybe you are trying to get a trustee on board with your plans. In which case you might need to show more specifically how it links to their obligations as a trustee.

3. BE SPECIFIC:

Getting your stakeholders to buy-in to your plans and primed to support you is one thing, but something I've noticed over the years is how much people assume it's obvious what is being asked of those stakeholders. You must bear in mind, however, that you have been involved in the whole marketing planning journey and hold all the detail that has led you to this point. Your stakeholders have not. Back in my corporate days, I remember the time I first shared my brand plan with a very trusted creative agency (under a non-disclosure agreement) so that they could see how their work fitted into my overall brand objectives. Even though we had worked together for many years, they found it an enlightening presentation and had plenty of questions for me. I still to this day recall the feeling of surprise that they didn't know more already. I had taken for granted that, since they had worked with me for so long, they knew my brands inside out. Of course I was only one of many clients, so they just weren't in the detail like I was.

Whether dealing with external or internal stakeholders, they will always have their own agendas, which means they just won't have the same focus on your projects that you do. Therefore

76

you need to be very specific and spell out exactly what is required of them, and by when. (Remember, some tasks may need to be actioned before another is able to commence).

The following table (also in the **workbook**) will help you capture the specifics:

WHO	THEIR INTEREST (WIFT)	ASK	WHEN

4. COMMUNICATE CLEARLY:

You will need to make sure that tasks are clearly communicated so everyone understands what is expected of them, and briefing is especially important when dealing with external parties. You should never assume they have understood what's required from a simple conversation. Always put it in writing so that you have something to measure and evaluate against later. By the same token, I would also strongly advise against pinging over a quick email brief without also having a discussion - so much can be lost without a conversation.

When using external suppliers, invest time to brief them thoroughly to ensure they fully understand what you are trying to achieve and how you want to achieve it. Putting in this time up front will save everyone time and money, as well as make you look professional, which in turn raises your suppliers' expectations of what they need to deliver to you!

Depending on the complexity of the task in hand, here are some tips on the key things you should include in a brief for an external supplier:

BRAND & PROJECT NAME: Your supplier is working on many projects at once, so provide a title to give the task focus

BACKGROUND: What are the important things to know about your organisation or this task? What made you decide to do this?

OBJECTIVE: What is the objective of the task? To launch a new website? To engage better? To re-brand? Attract a new audience?....

TARGET CUSTOMER(S): Who are you trying to attract? What do they think / feel about your brand now? And what do you want them to think / feel as a result of the work undertaken?

BRAND CONSIDERATIONS: What is the brand design, style, and tone that you are after?

PRACTICAL CONSIDERATIONS: Are there any practical considerations that should be included (e.g., technical, legal or specific things that haven't worked in the past)?

BUDGET: Be clear on how much you want to spend. If you really don't want to give anything away just yet, make sure you get a clear budget and breakdown of the output to approve before you proceed. This will avoid any nasty surprises later!

TIMING: What is your deadline and are there any particular milestones to meet (e.g.1st drafts required before a specific client or trustee meeting)? Make sure your supplier breaks the project down with dates.

THE BRIEF: What do you specifically want them to do? For instance, if building a website, do you also need them to create a logo, source visuals, copywrite etc? Or do you have the content collated and just need them to create the website structure, design and functionality.

OUTPUT: What is your expected output? In what format?

CONFIDENTIALITY: For anyone working on your organisation, make sure you have confidentiality in place for protection.

APPENDIX: This is an opportunity to refer your supplier to any existing work that gives them more background information about your business or project that will help them (e.g., brand guidelines, brand plan, competitor work, example work you like etc.).

What about me?

One of the many challenges small organisations face is personal time management. Often with resources tight, there are not enough hours in the day to do everything, which means inevitably the focus tends to be on getting through everything that keeps the operation running. However, if managing the day to day takes up too much time, there can be few or no hours to work on exciting new developments identified in your marketing plan.   This is where delegation can come in, either to other members of the team, or where there is budget, to external parties.   For those of you who have been there before, you will realise however, that it's not that simple because you still need to dedicate time to actually brief and manage that delegation! Finding the headspace for the extra projects that will develop your organisation can be tough, but unless you set aside the extra time, how will your organisation meet its objectives? It's all very well adding these tasks to the 'to-do' list, but how do you ensure you get to tick them off?

One tip I learned along the way, is to designate specific time in your week to these extra development projects. Find a time that suits you and stick with it. If you are an early bird, consider getting up earlier and allocating 1 hour every morning to work on new initiatives before you start your day. That's 5 hours a week, or 20 hours a month allocated to new projects. Perhaps you prefer the evening, or even the middle of the day as a refresher to break up your long hours. Do whatever is right for you and make it a habit. Block the time off in your calendar and let others around you know that you are not available.

REMINDERS – 'RESOURCES':

Remember:

- Allocate priorities to your tasks to simplify budget management and allow flexibility.

- Work through other people with clear communication of what needs doing and by when.

- Make space for your marketing by designating regular calendar time to work specifically on new initiatives.

PART 6

'T' = THE TIMING

In chapter 3, we discussed the importance of timing in setting your SMART(ER) goals. You also need to consider the timing of your marketing implementation to guarantee the end date for each marketing goal will be met.

Macro Timing – Big Picture

Firstly, look at the big picture to create an overview of all your marketing activities and map them out in a month by month planner:

- What activities need to take place and when? Are there key periods when it is important to launch / promote specific activities (these might be related to gifting seasons, seasonal trends, key business periods etc.)? Make sure you recognise any long lead-times, such as PR or advertising deadlines with media partners, or promotional calendar planning with wholesalers / retailers etc.

- Are any of your activities dependent on others happening first? Make sure you take these into account on your planner.

- What are the milestones for each activity? Make sure you break down your activities to manage the timing of sub-tasks. Long deadlines can easily end up parked in your mind, but they will end up delayed unless you recognise the timing for each step.

There are formal planning tools available for this, but a Excel simple spreadsheet will do the job nicely.

Micro Timing – Customer Detail

Once you have your monthly planner in place, it's time to think about the detail. This involves revisiting the customer journey and getting right into the specifics of timing and receptivity.

Just because you know where to find them, doesn't'

always mean your customers want to be found or disturbed. Get the timing wrong and they will not listen to you no matter how on point you are with your messaging. Imagine you have a range of organic healthcare products aimed at stay-at-home mothers to help them get back some 'me time'. In your planning, you may well choose Facebook or Instagram to reach them, but mothers are also busy and usually on a tight schedule, so you need to get your timing right. Catch them at the start of the day and they will be far too busy running a military operation to get everyone ready for school. Follow guidance from certain sources on when Facebook gets used the most and you might choose to post around 3pm - just when those mothers are now on the school run or racing to the next Scouts or ballet commitment. They are unlikely to be in the right frame of mind to think about their own wellbeing, meaning your post or advertisement will probably get unfairly swiped past. The same considerations come into play if you are running local radio advertising. Be careful not to be lured into cheaper late-night deals if your target audience is cosily tucked up in bed by 9.30!

There's no fixed science to finding the most receptive time per channel for your targets, so I suggest a common-sense approach and to think about how

85

you would feel if you were in their shoes. Then it's a matter of trial and error, reviewing what gets the best response and works best for your organisation.

Use your **workbook** to track your customer's daily (weekday and weekend) activities and receptivity (H=High, M=Medium, L=Low) to plan the best times to experiment with your posting.

TIME	ACTIVITY WEEKDAY / WEEKEND	RECEPTIVITY (H/M/L)
<6		
6 - 8		
8-10		
10-12		
ETC		

Commit to the Timing

There's no point putting all this marketing planning in place, if you then carry on without monitoring progress. Many things can get in the way of tasks being completed on time, and changes in market or business conditions may create new priorities. However, if that happens, it's important to see how that might affect your marketing goals. By tracking your performance, you can identify areas that should be addressed. Do you need to seek additional and / or external support? Or will a delay only have a minimal impact on your goals in which case you could simply change the deadline?

A useful way to do this is to colour code items using a traffic light system, which allows you to see at a glance the areas that need attention.

- RED: A milestone or deadline has been missed, so urgent action is required

- AMBER / ORANGE: The item is at risk of missing a milestone or deadline, so may need further support or be delayed

- GREEN: The activity is on track

This style of visual representation is particularly useful if working in a team as it provides focus during meetings and avoids time wasted discussing items that don't require your attention.

REMINDERS – 'TIMING':

Remember:

- Use a planner to time your marketing activities month by month to recognise key calendar milestones.

- Consider when your customer will be most receptive to your marketing.

- Monitor your activities to ensure you address and adjust any items at risk of impacting your marketing deadlines.

LISA WOODWARD

PART 7

BE CUSTOMER CENTRIC

Understand your Customer

The success of your marketing plan depends not only on your ability to set and reach well thought out marketing goals, but also on your ability to implement marketing activities that resonate with your potential customer. By customer, I mean whoever buys or uses your products or services; it could be your end consumer, a business customer, subscribers, or charity donor / volunteer etc.

You will have already identified your customer and where to reach them in your marketing plan. Now you need to think about how to make every piece of communication, compelling and relevant, and this

89

requires you to develop your understanding of them. The better you can imagine their world, the more poignant your marketing will become.

You may well need to target your marketing activities at more than one type of 'customer', in which case it is important to recognise their differences. Adapt your communication to only 'speak' with one type at a time. Otherwise, if you use the messages at once, you could struggle to resonate with them all. A good starting point is to create a customer persona for each.

Create a Customer Persona

Your customer persona is a fictional character who represents your **ideal** customer (note the **ideal**, this is not necessarily who you **currently** deal with). You want to gather as much information about them as possible so that you can find ways to appeal to them. That means not only noting their social demographic profile, but also gaining more emotive information so you connect your marketing messages to their behavioural triggers.

Start off with identifying their profile basics by asking as many questions as possible from the table below.

If you have existing customers, you can base this information on real knowledge and insights, otherwise do some desk research and try to visualise **yourself** as that ideal customer. You will find a template in your **workbook** to capture your persona information.

CUSTOMER PERSONA
Are they a B2C (consumer) or B2B (business) customer?
What is their age and gender?
What is their education / training?
What income bracket are they in?
What is their family situation?
Where do they live?
Where do they work? / What is their role?/ What do they do? / What are their ambitions?
What brands do they like? (& dislike!?)
What Media do they use? Press and social media. How do they interact with it (passively for research only or actively engaged)?
What are their key influences? (at home / work)
Where do they eat out? (social / at work)
What events do they attend? (personal / professional)
What are their hobbies / interests? (especially for B2C)
Are your products / services for them personally, gifts for others, or purchases made on behalf of a work team?
Other?

Some questions will be more relevant than others and you may wish to include further questions that are specific to your sector. Include anything might help you tailor a more poignant interaction.

Communicate at a More Emotional Level

Armed with this persona in mind, you will find it easier to, not only identify potential customer touchpoints (previously covered in Part 4), but also to gain an understanding of how your persona operates at an **emotional level.** This is key to successfully conveying the essence of what you do, because you need to connect the benefits of what your organisation offers with their emotional state, their motivations and frustrations. From your side, it is easy to see why your customers should buy into what you do, but you must explain 'why' from their standpoint and related to their needs in order to create compelling marketing messages that drive action.

Use my 3 P's template from your **workbook** to help uncover these needs. Simply imagine you are inside your ideal customer's mind and reflect on the following:

- Your **PASSIONS**: What are you motivated by? What do you seek in your personal or business life?

What are your ambitions?

- Your **PAINS**: What are your challenges, frustrations, or fears? What do you wish you could overcome? What could be your barriers to purchasing, signing up or donating?

Keep asking yourself 'why' to your answers to reach the root of your persona's passions and pains. This will uncover their deepest needs. (You can work through the same technique we used when looking at the issues coming out of your SWOT analysis in Part 2).

Next, answer how can you **POSITION** the benefits of your products or services against these insights. How do they meet these unmet needs and provide solutions for your persona? Get this right and your marketing will have much greater poignancy and impact than a rational list of benefits, because you are tapping directly into your persona's emotional needs.

PASSIONS	PAINS	POSITIONING
What are their **motivations** and **desires?**	What are their **challenges** and **fears?**	How will you position your **messages** to meet **these needs?**

You should also use testimonials or ratings from happy customers to boost your credibility and provide evidence of your organisation being able to deliver the promises you are making your ideal customer.

REMINDERS – 'BE CUSTOMER CENTRIC':

Remember:

- **Create a customer persona to understand your ideal customer so you can communicate with more relevance**

- **Always connect the rational benefits of what you offer to their emotional needs for more impactful marketing messages**

PART 8

A CIRCULAR PROCESS

Just the Start

Congratulations on completing your marketing plan. Hopefully you will have gained some clarity in deciding where to focus your efforts and resources. Remember, however, this is not a one-off exercise; marketing planning is a circular process. For the best results, take a step back and evaluate the impact of both your planning process and your marketing activities, so that you can learn and continue to improve the outcome of your marketing for the future.

See the Big Picture

There are a variety of business indicators you could use to see how you have performed against your goals. These might include data such as:

- your sales revenue growth, margin, return on investment
- market share, listings with retail suppliers
- number of new customers, repeat business
- donations or volunteer sign ups

These data will give you a good measure of how well your organisation has performed but will miss some of the learning opportunities for future planning. Therefore, it could also be beneficial to look specifically at your SMARTER goals and identify where things worked and where you could improve outcomes in future:

- SPECIFIC: Did you execute each goal as you specifically intended? Was the outcome as expected? What was the reaction of others (customers / competitors / team)? What worked well and what would you do again? What could you improve? What would you need to do to make that improvement?

- MEASURABLE: Did you meet your measurable target? What helped you? What hindered you? What would you repeat and what would you do differently?

- ACHIEVABLE: Were your goals stretching enough? Could you have gone further? Or were they too ambitious?

- RELEVANT: Did each goal fit with the overall purpose and strategy of the organisation? Was it relevant to the individuals or teams involved? What could have made it more relevant?

- TIME-BOUND: Did you reach your objective milestones on time? Where would you adjust timings in the future?

- ENJOYABLE: Did everyone involved enjoy the process? How could you engage them more willingly?

- RESPECTFUL: Was everyone involved respectful of other people, their roles, and organisational processes? Could anything be improved?

You can capture your learnings in your **workbook** template

Project Evaluation

As well as gaining a big picture review against your 3-4 goals, it is important to review how you got to your destination and whether there is anything you could learn at a more detailed executional level that would be useful for planning your future marketing initiatives. So, check each of your key marketing activities from part 4 and consider the 3 'O's:

OUTPUT	What has been delivered? Is it as expected? What could be better? How well did you stick to timings and budget?
OUTTAKE	What impact did your activity have on attitudes/ perceptions of your brand or organisation? (Customers / competitors etc.)
OUTCOME	What has happened or changed as a result of your activity. (Sales, listings, donations etc.) Remember it may only be small steps at a time as it can sometimes take a longer period of time to meet your objectives.

Now think about what you need to take into consideration for future planning. It can be easy to fall into the trap of doing what you've always done or what other stakeholders expect from you, but by going through this evaluation process and keeping your aims in mind, you can decipher what you need to work on. Use the STOP / START / CONTINUE template from chapter 3 (and from the downloadable **workbook**) to capture your learnings.

Conclusions

You will realise from the title of this chapter that marketing planning is not a one–off process. To be truly effective and maximise your chances of success, it needs to be circular. The world and local environment are constantly shifting so you should be reassessing your strategy on a regular basis. For the best chance of results, this requires continual evaluation and adjustment, revisiting your SWOT analysis at the end of each marketing period and setting new marketing goals based on the outcome of that review session. This should usually take place every 12 months, however in times of fast paced change you may need revisit it more often.

REMINDERS – 'A CIRCULAR PROCESS':

Remember:

- Use your business indicators to evaluate the success of your plan and review your SMARTER criteria for your objectives

- Regardless of how successfully you meet your business indicators, also review your implementation to see how you can improve effectiveness and efficiency in the future

- Marketing planning is not a one-off process. Use your learnings as input for your next cycle of planning

ABOUT THE AUTHOR

Lisa Woodward is an accomplished marketing professional, trainer and coach. Passionate about building brands to grow business for the long term, she believes that well thought out strategic thinking is an important recipe for success and should not be reserved for the brand elite who have the luxury of large marketing budgets.

Lisa spent much of her career amongst this elite, working over 20 years as a brand marketer in-house, developing and building iconic global brands such as TAG Heuer watches and Chivas Regal Scotch Whisky. It was during this time and whilst implementing her marketing plans through other internal and external teams, that she discovered her flair for creative thinking and ability to influence and motivate people at all levels within organisations. Wanting to use these skills to help others unravel the complexities of strategic thinking, she qualified as a coach and turned to a career in marketing coaching and consultancy.

In 2012, she set up her business, ICING Marketing, with the aim of bringing professional marketing know-how to micro businesses and SME's. The process in this book is based on the model Lisa uses in her client workshops and provides a framework and structure to build and implement well considered marketing plans without getting side swept by the demands of the day-to-day running of business; To keep a stubborn eye firmly on the end goal, always.

You can follow Lisa on social media:

FACEBOOK   @IcingMarketingUK
INSTAGRAM   **@IcingMarketingUK**
TWITTER   **@LisaIcing**

Or visit icingmarketing.com

Credit: Author photograph by Vicki Sharp

Also available
from the Think Simple Clever Series

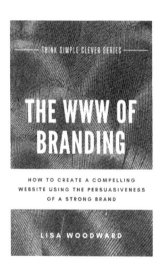

"Wow. Lisa Woodward cuts through the fluff and gets right to the heart of what needs to get done if you're going to build and market your own brand. Lisa gives you a play book on what to focus on and what to get done to give you and your brand the best shot. Her writing is crisp, concise, and lively. And, I love her real life examples from her own experiences…. Solid, solid read."

Edward Cole, President, Asia Pacific, Fender

With less than 15 seconds to make an impression on visitors to your website, the way in which you communicate your brand can dramatically improve your chances of turning a functionally competent website into one that is also relevant and captivating.

This book uniquely explains how to build a strong brand within the context of your website – a must for any organisation setting out to plan a new or refresh an existing website. Jargon free, its simple WWW model is a step-by-step approach that structures the clever but simple thinking you need to get your brand essentials in place before you go on-line.

Packed full of common-sense tools, this guide includes a useful downloadable workbook for your own planning - so that once you have enticed visitors to your site, your first impressions are more likely to translate into page impressions.

The WWW of Branding, available from Amazon
Published October 2020

SAMPLE TEMPLATES

A Word workbook containing editable templates is available for you to use to structure your marketing thinking. Download the workbook from:

https://www.icingmarketing.com/start

Alternatively, I have provided the templates here if you wish to make some notes to capture your initial thoughts from reading this guide.

Happy planning!

SITUATION
ANALYSIS

Where are you now?

STRENGTHS	WEAKNESSES

Opportunities	Threats

THEMES

Find the true themes from your SWOT and set your marketing goals

PROBLEM TREE TEMPLATE

ROOT CAUSE	DIRECT CAUSE	ISSUE	DIRECT CONSEQUENCE	END CONSEQUENCE	LIVE WITH Y/N?	CONTROL Y/N?
		Start here……				

GOAL SETTING

STOP	START	CONTINUE

SMARTER MARKETING GOALS		
1.		
2.		
3.		
4.		

ACTIONS

How will you reach your goals?

CUSTOMER TOUCHPOINTS

BEFORE	DURING	POST PURCHASE / EXPERIENCE

BEHAVE FAMOUSLY

FAMOUS BRAND OR PERSON	HOW WOULD THEY **APPROACH** THIS OBJECTIVE?	WHAT **CAN I TAKE** FROM THIS?

WHAT IF ....

WHAT ARE THE **BARRIERS?**	**WHAT IF** THAT BARRIER WASN'T THERE?

PRIORITISE THE ACTIONS

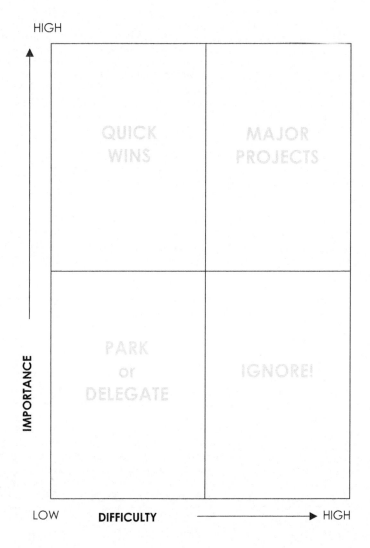

IDENTIFY THE DETAIL

OBJECTIVES (TO)	STRATEGY (BY)	CORE ACTIVITIES (DETAIL)	PRIORITY (1,2,3)
1.			
2.			
3.			
4.			

RESOURCES

How will you implement the plan?

IDENTIFY STAKEHOLDERS

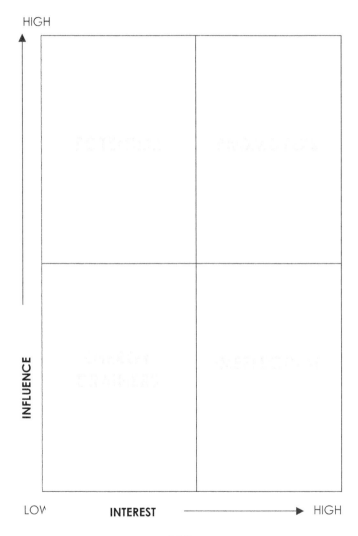

MANAGE STAKEHOLDERS

WHO	THEIR INTEREST (WIFT)	ASK	WHEN

TIMING

Plan the timing of your actions carefully

CUSTOMER RECEPTIVITY

TIME	ACTIVITY WEEKDAY	RECEPTIVITY (H/M/L)
<6		
6 - 8		
8-10		
10-12		
12-14		
14-16		
16-18		
18-20		
20-24		

TIME	ACTIVITY WEEKEND	RECEPTIVITY (H/M/L)
<6		
6 - 8		
8-10		
10-12		
12-14		
14-16		
16-18		
18-20		
20-24		

BE CUSTOMER CENTRIC

Ensure everything is relevant and connects with your ideal customer

CUSTOMER PERSONA
Are they a B2C (consumer) or B2B (business) customer?
What is their age range / gender?
What is their education / training?
What income bracket are they in?
What is their family situation?
Where do they live?
Where do they work? / What is their role?/ What do they do? / What are their ambitions?
What brands do they like? (& dislike!?)
What Media do they use? (Press and social media) How do they interact with it (passively for research or actively engaged)?

What are their key influences? (at home / work)

Where do they eat out? (social / at work)

What events do they attend? (personal / professional)

What are their hobbies / interests? (especially for B2C)

Are your products / services for them personally, gifts for others, or purchases made on behalf of a work team?

Other?

PASSIONS	PAINS	POSITIONING
What are their **motivations** and **desires?**	What are their **challenges** and **fears?**	How will you position your **messages** to meet **these needs?**

A CIRCULAR PROCESS

Evaluate to learn and plan for the future

REVIEW THE PLAN AGAINST EACH OBJECTIVE

OBJECTIVE ....

WAS IT?	DETAIL
SPECIFIC	
MEASURABLE	
ACHIEVABLE	
RELEVANT	
TIME-BOUND	
ENJOYABLE	
RESECTFUL	

PROJECT EVALUATION

OUTPUT	How was the delivery?
OUTTAKE	What was the impact?
OUTCOME	What has resulted from it?

Thank you for reading!

Please add a short review on Amazon and let me know whether you found this book useful.

Printed in Great Britain
by Amazon